W9-CAR-977

CHRISTMAS TREEVIA

By
D. Peter Harrington

HARRINGTON COMPANIES, WAYZATA, MINNESOTA

COPYRIGHT BY

D. PETER HARRINGTON

1994

TX-3-618-534

THIS BOOK
PUBLISHED BY
HARRINGTON COMPANIES
WAYZATA, MINNESOTA

ALL RIGHTS RESERVED

PRINTED IN THE UNITED STATES

SECOND EDITION

Typography and Printing by the Crepeau Company

PREFACE:

When the Holidays come, do you ever ask yourself any of the following questions?

Why do we bring evergreens and holly into the house during the holidays?

Why do we celebrate Christmas in December when it is thought by many historians that Christ was born during the summer?

Where did the fruitcake come from?

Why are there the twelve days of Christmas?

These questions and many more are answered in this book, "CHRISTMAS TREEVIA."

INTRODUCTION:

CHRISTMAS TREEVIA
A BOOK OF TRIVIA ON HOLIDAY TRADITIONS

Most holiday traditions came to the United States
with the English, who had been influenced by the
Germans. These traditions originated with the
Romans and Ancient Greeks, and were passed down
through various ancient cultures. Our traditions grew
out of agricultural societies where the culture's
success depended on the crops that could be grown.
 Ancient societies celebrated the winter solstice on
December 21st, the shortest day of the year, with
festive activities that usually involved the worship of
their sun god. Fires, candles, and prayers for the sun
to return for another growing season were used in
these festivities. After these celebrations, the days
became longer and it was clear that a new growing
season had started. Christian traditions and beliefs
were easily adapted from these ancient celebrations.

COPYRIGHT 1994
ALL RIGHTS RESERVED

TABLE OF CONTENTS

Health, Peace, and sweet content be yours.
Shakespeare

A

A.D.

Anno Domini, from the Latin meaning, "In the year of the Lord." Most , societies today start their dating system with the year Christ was born. In 532 A.D., the monk, Dionysius Exiguis, started the Christian system of dating based on the year he believed Christ was born. Anything that occurred after his birth is A.D., anything before is B.C., before Christ. Jesus was believed to be born in the Roman year of 747.

ADVENT:

Derived from the Latin word "adventus" meaning "to come." In the Christian Church, it is the four weeks before Christmas, starting on the Sunday nearest St. Andrews Day, November 30. It has been celebrated since the sixth century as a preparation for the celebration of the birth of Christ and his second coming.

ADVENT CALENDAR:

A calendar starting on Advent Sunday and lasting through Christmas. Many calendars have windows, with surprises or pictures behind them, that a child can open each day until Christmas. The pictures depict a Christmas story.

ADVENT CANDLES:

Candles that are lit, one each Sunday during Advent, until all the candles are lit by the Sunday before Christmas.

ADVENT SUNDAY: The first Sunday in Advent.

A
ADVENT WREATH:

Originally from Germany, it is an evergreen wreath, usually hung horizontally and decorated with red, gold or purple ribbons. The four advent candles are attached to the wreath.

ALBERT, PRINCE:

Prince Albert was Queen Victoria's German husband. It was because of him that a Christmas tree was placed in Windsor Castle in 1841. He wanted his children to enjoy one of his favorite Christmas traditions from childhood. This was the start of the Christmas tree becoming popular in England.

ANDREW, SAINT:

St. Andrew was one of the twelve disciples. His saints feast day is held on November 30th. Advent always starts on the Sunday following this day.

ARCHBISHOP AUGUSTINE:

In the 6th century, Pope Gregory I asked Augustine, the first Archbishop of Canterbury, to incorporate as many local and ancient customs, which were capable of Christian interpretation, into English religious society. By the Middle Ages, at Christmas time, holly berries, formerly used as a holiday decoration by the Druids, had come to symbolize the Blood of Christ, the prickly leaves, The Crown of Thorns, and clinging ivy, Immortality.[1]

B

BAH-HUMBUG:

Something that is done to deceive or cheat someone. Something said that is misleading or made up of empty talk. A hoax.

BALTHASAR:

One of the three Wise Men. He was a tall black skinned man and was the King of Ethiopia. His gift to the Christ Child was Myrrh, representing Christ's suffering. He is depicted as a bearded man in his 40's.

BETHLEHEM:

A Hebrew word for house. It is an ancient town in Palestine believed to be the birthplace of Christ. Today it has a population of about 30,000 people and is located in the country of Jordan.

BOAR'S HEAD:

In early English celebrations, the Christmas feast was started by the entrance of a Boar's head with an apple or lemon in its mouth, carried aloft to the King's table while harps played and carols were sung. The head itself was deboned and coated with minced pig's liver, chopped apples, sage, onions and rosemary. Then the head was stuffed with sausage meat, ox tongue, truffles, mushrooms, pistachios, nuts and spices, all moistened with apple brandy. It was boiled for a day before it was served.[2]

B

BOUGH:

The branch of a tree such as an evergreen bough, or a bough of holly.

BOXING DAY:

The day after Christmas, on December 26th, tradesmen are given gifts of money by their employers. Also food and clothing are given to the poor by churches and charities. This is still a custom in England and Canada. It all started in the Middle Ages with an "Alms Box," which was placed at the door of a church. There was only one opening in the earthenware box, large enough for money to be deposited. It was always broken open on December 26th, and the money was distributed among the poor. In Holland and Germany a similar custom existed with children. They put their money into an earthenware box in the form of a pig. This container was called the "feast pig," and it was broken open on Christmas. This is the early version of the "piggy bank."

C

CAESAR AUGUSTUS:

The Roman ruler that made the decree that all men should be taxed, each in his own city. Therefore, Joseph and Mary had to go to Bethlehem to pay their taxes. It was here that Christ was born.

CANDY CANE:

A cane usually made of red and white hard candy. It is thought that it originates from the staff that was carried by St. Nicholas or by the shepherds.

CAROLS:

Christmas carols came from France about 1300 A.D. There were abolished in England, as well as Christmas celebrations, by Oliver Cromwell and the Puritans in the mid 1600s. It was not until the mid 1800s, during the Victorian period in England, that carols again became a tradition. For many years they were only sung outside the church, as the clergy frowned upon them. But, they remained popular and eventually were sung in the church because the common man could relate to them. The original carols were a bit on the bawdy side.

CHRIST:

A word that comes from the Greek meaning "the anointed one" or "The Messiah." Originally it was a title, as in Jesus the Christ or the Messiah. Later it became the name Jesus Christ.

C

CHRISTMAS:

CHRIST & MASS. Christmas is the feast of the birth of Jesus Christ. It is thought to be an important occurrence, but it was not celebrated on December 25th until 336 A.D., when Pope Julius decided to create a festival celebrating the birth of Christ, to counteract the pagan festivities connected with the winter solstice. It is actually thought that Christ was born during the summer months, as that would be the time the shepherds would be tending their flocks of sheep. The Romans had celebrated the feast of the "Invincible Sun" on December 25th since 274 B.C. The Eastern Christian churches preferred January 6th as the day of celebration, but agreed with December 25th when they decided to celebrate the feast of Epiphany on January 6, the day the "Wise Men" were introduced to the Christ Child. The Puritans, in England, Europe, and New England tried to abolish Christmas because of its pagan connections, but the move was unpopular and Christmas survived.

CHRISTMAS CARDS:

The first Christmas cards were produced in 1843 by John Horsley. He also designed the first postage stamp in England. He sold about 1000 cards the first year. The first card showed three generations of a family drinking wine. The original tradition was to send a "Christmas piece," a few lines written to friends on fancy paper, to let them know how their family was doing, similar to today's "Christmas letter." It was an established tradition in England by 1880. It is thought that Annie Oakley was the first person in America to send a Christmas Card.

"A CHRISTMAS CAROL":

Charles Dickens' tale of Ebenezer Scrooge, a miser who is transformed by love and fear into a lovable character who has compassion for his fellow man. Written in 1843, Dickens was making a statement on the conditions in London of the poor and unfortunate. He is given much of the credit for making Christmas popular again after the reign of the Puritans from the mid 1600s to the mid 1800s.

C

CHRISTMAS COLORS:

The traditional colors of red and green more than likely had their origins from pagan times when boughs of holly were brought into the house for good luck, during the winter solstice. The leaves were green and the berries red. Later, when Christmas trees were decorated, people used red apples, as they represented the apple in the Adam and Eve portion in the "Mystery Play."

CHRISTMAS CRACKERS:

Christmas crackers are a sugared almond wrapped with a material that, when unwrapped, bangs like a firecracker. Invented by Thomas Smith in the mid 1800s, they have been exported throughout the British Empire but have never become popular in the United States.

CHRISTMAS DECORATIONS:

Christmas trees were originally decorated with gilded fruit apples, nuts, sweets, and paper roses. Candles were used to illuminate the tree, which have now been replaced by electric lights invented in the late 1890s. The first glass ornaments were imported from Germany in the 1880s.

CHRISTMAS GIFTS:

The giving of gifts can be traced back to Roman times when it was a tradition to give the emperor a gift on New Year's Day. St. Nicholas is given much credit for bringing gift-giving to Christmas. It was not until the middle of the 19th century that it became a tradition to give gifts on Christmas Day to commemorate the giving of gifts by the three kings. Until this century, Christmas gifts were not extravagant. They were modest and consisted of fruit, small toys for children, and homemade works of art, such as needle work. Adults also gave each other almanacs, yearly calendars with useful information, such as weather forecasts.

C

CHRISTMAS TREE:

The Christmas tree was originally a German custom. It was thought by pagan religions that bringing evergreens into the house during the festival of the winter solstice would bring good luck. The evergreen was chosen because it is one of the only trees that seems to be alive during the winter. The custom spread to England during the reign of Queen Victoria, who was married to the German Prince Albert.
He wanted to have his children enjoy one of his childhood memories. Queen Victoria had a Christmas tree in Windsor Castle in 1841. It had become a custom throughout England by 1860. In Germany and in ancient northern cultures, after the festivities, the branches were removed and the trunk was decorated on May 1st as a May Pole, celebrating a rebirth of spring. The tree was then cut up and the largest log was used the next December as the Yule log. The first Christmas tree was thought to have appeared in a "Mystery Play" during the middle ages. Another theory is that Martin Luther, when walking through the woods on a clear winter night, decided to bring a tree inside the house so his children could enjoy its beauty.

CHURCH, FRANCIS:

Francis Church worked for the New York Sun Newspaper. He is the columnist that answered Virginia O'Hanlon's letter. His article was entitled "Yes Virginia, there is a Santa."

CITY OF DAVID:

The same as Bethlehem. It was the City of King David.

COURSERS:

A word found in the poem by Clement Moore, "A Visit from St. Nick," which states, "the coursers they flew." The word refers to a team of graceful, swift horses and in this case refers to a team of reindeer.

15

C

CRANBERRIES:

The cranberry is one of the only foods from America that is now a traditional sauce or relish with a holiday Christmas dinner.

CRATCHIT FAMILY:

The family of Bob Cratchit, the clerk who worked for Ebenezer Scrooge in Dickens' "A Christmas Carol." He had a wife, always referred to as Mrs. Cratchit. His oldest daughter was Martha, his second daughter was Belinda, his oldest son was Master Peter and his crippled son was Tiny Tim. He had two younger children only referred to as the two young Cratchits, a boy and a girl.

CRECHE:

A display of a stable with figures representing the birth of Christ, usually displayed at Christmas. It was introduced by St. Francis of Assisi in Italy in 1224.

CROMWELL, OLIVER:

Oliver Cromwell defeated King Charles in 1648 and established Puritanism. This government lasted until 1659 when his son Richard Cromwell was forced by the English army to abdicate. The government was again returned to the Crown; but the Puritans controlled religious matters, and it was not until the middle 1800s that Christmas again became popular. During the reign of the Puritans, Christmas was all but outlawed. On Christmas Day, stores had to remain open and churches were closed!

D

DICKENS, CHARLES:

Charles Dickens published yearly Christmas stories starting in 1843 with "A Christmas Carol" which is the best known of these Christmas tales. This story was originally published as a serial in the newspaper. Throughout his life he wrote novels, helped to establish a home for reformed prostitutes, pressed for slum clearance, education reforms, sanitary measures, and other social issues that appear in his works. He was born in England in 1812 and died in 1870. He is given much credit for making Christmas popular again after its demise during the Middle Ages under the watch of the Puritan Reformers.

DRUIDS:

The ancient pagan cult that lived in England and Europe before the Romans conquered it in 66 A.D. were called the Celts. Many people believed they built Stonehenge, an ancient temple made of huge stone pillars, that still stands in England, although this fact has never been proven. The priests of the Celts were called Druids. They worshiped gods of nature, believed in immortality and reincarnation, and were astronomers. They used evergreens, ivy, and holly to decorate their temples during the period of the winter solstice which are now used at Christmas time as decorations. Their main religious rite involved the oak tree from which they cut mistletoe with a gold knife. It was believed that mistletoe would keep evil spirits and witches away.

E

EGGNOG:

A cold drink made with rum. eggs, milk, nutmeg. and sugar. Its origins are related to the Tom and Jerry and to a rum sauce called Cumberland sauce that was poured over cake and eaten at the time of a birth in northern England, to wish a newborn well. All have similar ingredients.

ELVES:

In Norway, Christmas elves were called "Julenisse." They are legendary creatures who are given a bowl of rommegrot on Christmas Eve. They are thought to live in the barn and help the entire household throughout the year. It is thought that this is the beginning of the myth that Santa Claus has elves that help him make toys. The Swedish believe in a similar gnome-like elf that also lives in the barn and helps the farmer. They are called "Jultomter."

EMMANUEL (IMMANUEL):

A word derived from the Hebrew meaning "God is with us." It is used to refer to Christ. It also means an appearance of God or any other supernatural being.

EPIPHANY:

Epiphany is a Christian Feast celebrated on January 6th. The word comes from the Greek meaning "appearance" or "revelation." This is the day that the Christ Child was introduced to the gentiles in the form of the Magi or "Three Wise Men." During the Middle Ages it was also the twelfth day of Christmas which was the most festive day of the Christmas Holidays.

F

SAINT FRANCIS OF ASSISI:

St. Francis is given credit for introducing the creche in Italy in 1224. He placed the first creche in his church so that the Christmas story might be more easily understood by his people as most were unable to read. It was very unusual compared to the strict methods used by the church at that time. It aroused a new spirit and interest in Christmas that spread throughout Europe.

FRANKINCENSE:

An aromatic resin obtained from the Boswellia tree in the African country of Somalia and in the southern peninsula of Arabia. It was a prized commodity and traded throughout Persia, for religious and medicinal purposes. The gum is an ingredient of fumigants and perfume and can be burned as incense. It is obtained by cutting a deep incision in the trunk of the tree which allows a milky juice to flow. When air hits the juice, it hardens into a semi-opaque lump which is the product that was traded.

FRUITCAKE:

The fruitcake was the original dessert at the English feast on the Twelfth Day of Christmas or Epiphany. Somehow it has lasted, and is believed by some that one of the original cakes is still given out at Christmas by someone that received it for a gift the Christmas before.

G

GARLAND:

Garlands are swags or sprays made of evergreen branches wired together and hung inside the house as decorations. It is thought the origin is probably from the Druids, who believed that this would bring good luck to the household. Today, they are made of many different materials and are used to decorate Christmas trees.

GASPER (CASPER also KASPER):

One of the three "Wise Men." His gift to the Christ Child was frankincense. He was the King of Tarus and was a tall, beardless man in his 20's.

GOOSE:

The Christmas goose, which is roasted until its skin is golden brown and crisp, is still popular in England and has been since the Middle Ages. In the time of Charlemagne, geese were a prized food and were used to pay property taxes. The goose is described in Dickens', "A Christmas Carol" with the phrase, "there never has been such a goose." Many times goose is served with no fancy trimmings, only two side dishes of applesauce and mashed potatoes with a goose gravy.

H

HALLOWEEN:

On October 31st, at the Halloween festival, the Lord of Misrule was elected to rule during the coming Christmas season. This was an occasion of great feasting and merry making. It was stopped in the mid 1600s when the Puritans gained power, and was never reestablished.

HARRISON, BENJAMIN:

Benjamin Harrison was the first President of the United States to set the pattern for Christmas festivities at the White House. He was President from 1889 to 1893.

HERALD ANGELS:

An angel who delivers the news. The shepherds tending their flocks were told of the birth of Christ by the Herald Angels. Many newspapers use the name Herald because it means a person who announces significant news.

HEROD:

King Herod was the Roman king in Judea at the time Christ was born. He was told of the star in the east and of the birth of the King of the Jews by the Wise Men. He then told the Wise Men to find the baby so he could come and worship him. The Wise Men followed the star and found the Christ Child. They were warned by God, in a dream, not to return to Herod, and they did not. Joseph was also warned by an angel of God, in a dream, to take the child and his mother into Egypt because Herod was to seek out the child and kill him. Shortly after Joseph left with his family, Herod ordered the massacre of all the infants in Bethlehem. This was shortly before Herod's death. After he had died, the angel again appeared to Joseph and told him to return to Israel. He and his family returned to Nazareth.

H

HOLIDAY:

HOLY & DAY. A day set aside for holy worship. It now means any day that is taken away from work for purposes of worship, celebration, or recreation.

HOLLY:

Holly was used by the Druids, the priests of the pagan Celtics in England, to decorate their homes and temples. It was thought to be magical because it retained its leaves and bore its fruit in the winter. It is the most obvious pagan relic whose use has been transferred to Christmas. By the Middle Ages, holly was used to decorate churches in England. The red berries symbolized the Blood of Christ, and the prickly leaves, the Crown of Thorns.

HOSANNA:

A word that means "Save, We Pray." It is an exclamation of praise to God.

J

JEHOVAH:

A word that means "My Lord or God."

JERUSALEM:

The capital of Israel and the religious center of three religions, Christianity, Judaism, and Islam. It is the city where Christ was put to death by Pontius Pilate.

JESUS:

A word derived from the Hebrew meaning "to help" or "the help of God." It was a masculine name in biblical times. Mary and Joseph named him Jeshau, a common Hebrew name meaning "the Lord is salvation." The Greek form is Jesus.

JOSEPH:

The husband of Mary, the mother of Christ. He is given much attention in the first two chapters of Matthew and Luke, and is portrayed as a carpenter in Nazareth, a descendant of Bethlehem's David, and was a kind husband and father. The Catholic Church made him the Saint of Workers, for his faithful cooperation in the birth of Christ.

JUDAEA:

The southern portion of ancient Palestine, now part of Israel. Jerusalem was in Judaea.

KISSING BALL:

The kissing ball was popular in England and still is. It probably was derived from the wreath with mistletoe, but was an easier item to hang in doorways and other places where a woman could be kissed. It is made with evergreens, ornaments, and mistletoe. It is usually small, no more than eight inches round, maybe so a woman won't notice!

KRIS KRINGLE:

In Germany, during the reformation, St. Nicholas was replaced by a gift-bearing figure, a harbinger of the Christ Child about to be born. The child was usually a girl called "Christkindal," which eventually was changed to Kris Kringle.

L

LITTLE JACK HORNER:

In the nursery rhyme "Little Jack Horner," Jack was eating a Christmas pie. That pie would have been a mincemeat pie.

LOWING:

A term that is found in the song "Away in the Manger." It was believed that at midnight on Christmas Eve, the animals would bow down in reverence to Christ and speak in human tongues.

SAINT LUCIA'S DAY:

This day is celebrated in Sweden on December 13th. At dawn, the youngest girl in the house, dressed in a white flowing gown tied with a red sash and with a crown of lighted candles on her head, serves coffee and Lucia buns (shaped like a cat's head) to everyone in the house that she awakens. Lucia was originally a beautiful Roman maiden who refused to renounce her Christianity and was burned at the stake. Because it falls on December 13th, when the days are short, it is an occasion to light candles.

LUMINARIES:

Luminaries are small lanterns that light walkways and are set out at Christmas time. They originated in Spain and Old Mexico. They are now made of paper bags with candles or electric lights inside. Their original intent was to guide Mary and Joseph on a safe journey.

LUTEFISK (LYE-FISH):

A Scandinavian dish of cod fish that has been soaked in lye, then rinsed, cooked, and is served with melted butter or a cream sauce. It is popular with Scandinavian people as a Holiday dish. In Norway, cod is still caught during spawning season between January and April and is dried in the winter cold. It has been a Norwegian trading commodity for centuries.

M

MAGI:

The Magi were the priestly hierarchy of the ancient religion, Zoroastrianism, the state religion of Persia. They were keepers of the cult and sacrificial power and were powerfully active in politics. They were thought to be astrologers who were able to interpret dreams, and therefore were considered "Wise Men." The word magic is derived from this term. The name came to be applied to the "Wise Men from the East," who followed the star of Bethlehem to become the first gentiles to believe in Christ. The Christians celebrate their visit with the feast of the Epiphany on January 6th, or the twelfth day of Christmas. The "Wise Men" brought gifts of gold, frankincense, and myrrh. The Bible never mentions how many "Wise Men" visited, but only mentions the three gifts. It was later thought that they represented the three phases of life. Casper was youth, Balthasar was middle age, and Melchoir was elderly.

MANGER:

A wooden trough or box, filled with hay, from which cattle and horses eat.

MARLEY, JACOB:

The dead partner of Ebenezer Scrooge in Dickens', "A Christmas Carol."

M

MARY:

Mary, the mother of Jesus Christ, has been given a special place in the Christian Church, especially in the Catholic and Eastern Orthodox Churches. The New Testament remarks that she was the cousin of Elizabeth, the mother of John the Baptist. The New Testament says that Mary conceived Jesus by the Holy Ghost, and therefore remained a Virgin. The doctrine of Mary's "Immaculate Conception" was disputed throughout the Middle Ages. It was formally established as doctrine in 649 by the church's Latern Council. The idea that Mary remained a perpetual virgin is taught principally by the Catholic and Orthodox churches. In 1854, Pope Pius IX declared that Mary was freed of original sin, but it was not until 1950 that it became an official doctrine of the Catholic Church, under Pope Pius XII who reigned as Pope from 1939 to 1958.

MAYPOLE:

The Maypole was made from the trunk of the Christmas tree. When the tree was taken out of the house on January 6th, its branches were removed so that it could be used as the Maypole. In the spring, on May 1st, the pole was decorated with ribbons and flowers to celebrate the coming of spring.

MELCHOIR:

Melchoir was one of the Magi or one of "The Three Kings." His gift to Christ was gold representing Royalty. He was a small, older man and the King of Nubia.

MESSIAH:

The promised liberator and savior of the Jews. Jesus is regarded as the realization of the "Messianic" prophecy in the Christian Religion.

M

MINCEMEAT:

Mincemeat was originally made from minced meat, usually mutton, and mixed with fruit. Over the years the meat has totally been replaced by the fruit. The original pies were made in the shape of a crib and exchanged on Christmas Eve. When your family received a mince pie it meant they would have good luck for one month, therefore it was necessary to give and receive twelve pies to insure a full year of good luck.[3]

MISRULE:

Before the Puritans came to power, a Lord of Misrule and his court, were elected on Halloween to rule over the following Christmas festivities. The Lord and his court would make fun of the aristocrats, which was tolerated. They would even make fun of the church! This was similar to a Roman celebration called "Saturnalia" where the slaves were given the right to do and say whatever they wanted. In Misrule activities, masks were used and it became a time for riotous and disorderly revels. The Lord of Misrule was the main celebrity in Medieval Christmas celebrations. When the Puritans took over, they banned this part of the Christmas celebration forever. The only remnant that remains today is found in the armed forces where the officers serve their men Christmas dinner.

MISTLETOE:

Mistletoe was used by the Druids, the priests of the pagan Celtic culture in England, to decorate their homes and their temples during the winter solstice. It was thought to be magical because it was one of the only plants that bore its fruit during the winter. It was cut from oak trees with a golden knife. Because it had been treasured so highly by the Druids, it was considered too pagan and sinful and is still forbidden by some churches today. Kissing under the mistletoe is purely an English custom. The white berry of the mistletoe is poisonous. It was thought to have magical powers and would keep away witches and evil spirits.

M

MITER:

An ornamental hat that is worn by the Pope, Bishops, or Abbots. It is believed that the hat Santa Claus wears was designed after the miter worn by the Dutch bishops.

MOORE, CLEMENT CLARK:

Clement Moore was a bible and Hebrew scholar at the Episcopalian Institution in New York City. He was born in 1779 and died in 1863. He is most famous for writing the poem, "A Visit from St. Nicholas," in 1824 which begins "Twas the night before Christmas. ..." He is given credit for developing the myth that Santa Claus rode in a sleigh pulled by eight reindeer and giving those reindeer names.

MYRRH:

The myrrh tree grows from 4 to 20 feet high and has a very large trunk. Myrrh is extracted from the tree by tapping it and allowing the yellow fluid to drain and be collected in lumps known as tears. It was exported from Arabia and Somalia, as its oil was used to make perfume.

MYSTERY PLAYS:

During the 14th and 15th centuries, when most people were illiterate, the church initiated these plays during the time of the winter solstice celebrations, to educate the peasants on the Bible and the life of Christ. These plays used ancient trappings such as evergreens and ivy. It is thought that the Christmas tree originated in one of these plays, decorated with apples, depicting the apple in the story of Adam and Eve. They were also called "Miracle Plays." During these plays, songs were sung during interludes. If the songs were liked, the singers would march into the streets singing them, therefore becoming the first carolers.

NATIVITY:

A word used to describe the birth of Jesus Christ. It is derived from the Latin word "nativitas" meaning birth.

NAZARETH:

After 40 days and nights, Mary and Joseph left Bethlehem for exile in Egypt because of King Herod. Nazareth was the city to which Mary and Joseph returned after Jesus was two years old and King Herod had died. They lived there quietly and humbly with their family.

NOEL:

A word that means Christmas or Christmas Carol. It comes from the Latin word, "natalis," which means the day of birth.

NORTH POLE:

The home of Santa Claus. It is not clear where this myth started, but it is probably of Scandinavian origin.

NUTCRACKER:

The origin of the nutcracker in the shape of a toy soldier came from "The Nutcracker Suite," by Tchaikovsky. Toy soldiers are very common at Christmas time because of this ballet written in 1892. It is about a little girl who wishes that her nutcracker, in the form of a toy soldier, would become a live prince.

P

PATRICK, SAINT:

St. Patrick is credited with bringing Christmas to Ireland.

PIERCE, FRANKLIN:

President Pierce had the first Christmas tree in the White House in 1856.

PIGGY BANK:

In Holland and Germany the piggy bank was derived from "Boxing Day." An earthen container shaped like a pig was broken open at Christmas time to retrieve the money which was given to the poor.

PLUM PUDDING:

Plum pudding was originally a porridge in Medieval times, made with meat broth, spices, and wine, all thickened with brown bread crumbs. At that time, it was eaten at the beginning of the meal. It was not until the 18th century that it became a round ball of pudding boiled in a cloth and eaten as a dessert. Silver coins and trinkets were added to the pudding when it was made. The pudding was always made the Sunday before Christmas. Everyone in the family was to stir it to bring them good luck, therefore it was called "Stir up Sunday." The person who got the silver coin in their portion of pudding was promised great wealth. A silver ring prophesied a speedy wedding, while a thimble meant a girl was to become an old maid.[4]

POINSETTIA:

An ornamental shrub that is native to Mexico, and became popular at Christmas because of its green and red color. It was brought to the United States by the first ambassador to Mexico, Dr. Joel Poinsette of South Carolina, in 1852. He was a botanist and started to cultivate the plant in the United States.[5]

R

REINDEER:

A large deer found in the European and North American tundra. In America it is called the Caribou. The legend of Santa Claus having a sleigh pulled by eight reindeer originated in the poem by Clement Moore, "A Visit from St. Nick." He also gave them their names, Dasher, Dancer, Prancer, Vixen, Comet, Cupid, Donder, and Blitzen.

ROBIN'S RED BREAST:

It was believed that on the night of the Nativity, a Robin had fanned the infant Jesus with his wings to keep him warm, and in doing so had gotten too close to the flame and burned his chest.[6]

ROMMEGROT:

A Scandinavian holiday dessert made with flour, butter and cream.

RUDOLPH, the Red Nosed Reindeer:

Rudolph, the Red Nosed Reindeer became popular in the 1950s when a song, written in 1949 by Johnny Marks and sung by Gene Autry, became popular. Since that time it is thought that on cloudy and foggy Christmas nights, Rudolph guides Santa's sleigh with his bright red nose. The song was based on a story written for Montgomery Ward and Company in 1939. The song was Columbia Record's all time best seller. By 1950 it had sold over one million copies and today has sold over ninety-one million copies world wide. It is runner up in sales to the all time best hit, "White Christmas." It was Gene Autry's biggest hit. He introduced it at Madison Square Garden in 1949.

S

SAINT NICHOLAS:

St. Nicholas, the patron saint of Russia, was a bishop of the church around 350. He was known for his great generosity and compassion. He is also the patron saint of children and sailors. He is best remembered for saving three daughters of a destitute nobleman from a life of prostitution. On three different occasions, he tossed a bag of gold through their window to provide a dowry so that each daughter could enter into an honorable marriage. Variations of his name range from Sant Nikolaas, to Sante Claas or Santa Claus. In England he is known as Father Christmas, Grandfather Frost in Russia, Pere Noel in France, St. Nick in Holland, and Santa Claus in the United States.

SANTA CLAUS:

Santa Claus is the American adaptation of St. Nicholas, a legendary European figure that brings presents to children on Christmas Eve. The name Santa Claus is derived from the Dutch, "Sinter Class." Originally, St. Nicholas brought presents to children on December 6th, the feast day of St. Nicholas, but in the United States it was changed to December 25th. The main features of Santa Claus can be attributed to the Dutch. They said he came down the chimney and left switches for bad children instead of presents. The red suit trimmed with white fur and the red cap were copied by the Dutch from their Bishop's cape and miter, or hat. The reindeer and sleigh originated in the poem by Clement Moore, "A Visit from St. Nick."

SAVIOR:

One who saves or delivers. When the word is capitalized it means "Jesus Christ."

S

SHEPHERDS:

On the night Christ was born, the angel of the Lord came to the shepherds who were watching over their flocks. The angel said, "fear not; for behold, I bring you good tidings of great joy, which shall be to all people. For unto you is born this day, in the city of David, a saviour, which is Christ the Lord. And this shall be a sign unto you. Ye shall find the babe wrapped in swaddling clothes, lying in a manger." The shepherds were the first to visit the Christ Child. They started spreading the news of his birth.

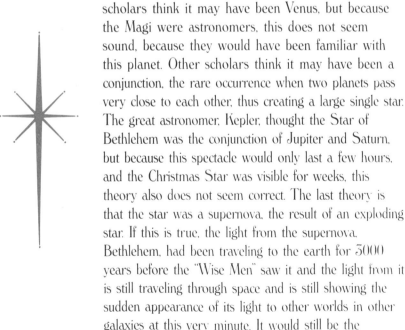

STAR OF BETHLEHEM:

The Star of Bethlehem is also known as the Christmas Star or The Star of the East. Many theories exist as to what it actually was. Some scholars think it may have been Venus, but because the Magi were astronomers, this does not seem sound, because they would have been familiar with this planet. Other scholars think it may have been a conjunction, the rare occurrence when two planets pass very close to each other, thus creating a large single star. The great astronomer, Kepler, thought the Star of Bethlehem was the conjunction of Jupiter and Saturn, but because this spectacle would only last a few hours, and the Christmas Star was visible for weeks, this theory also does not seem correct. The last theory is that the star was a supernova, the result of an exploding star. If this is true, the light from the supernova, Bethlehem, had been traveling to the earth for 5000 years before the "Wise Men" saw it and the light from it is still traveling through space and is still showing the sudden appearance of its light to other worlds in other galaxies at this very minute. It would still be the brightest star in any world's sky today because of its enormous size and light. Some theologians think the star may have been an angel guiding the Wise Men.

S

STOCKING, CHRISTMAS:

The Christmas stocking originated with St. Nicholas in Russia about 350 A.D. A nobleman had lost his money in a bad business investment which put his three daughters in the position of not having a dowry and therefore they would not be able to be married. They faced a possible life of prostitution! On three different occasions, Bishop Nicholas threw a bag of gold through their window to save them from this destiny. On one of these occasions the bag fell into one of their stockings left hanging by the fire to dry and the custom began. In the United States, stockings were the best known tradition until the advent of the Christmas tree in the late 1800s. By 1900 decorative stockings were sold as well as pre-stuffed stockings.[7]

SUGAR PLUM:

The sugar plum is a round or oval piece of sugary candy. It can also be a bonbon, which is a chocolate covered cream.

SWADDLING CLOTHES:

Long narrow bands of cloth wrapped around a newborn infant in ancient times that would restrict the baby's movement. It was thought that this would keep the baby contented.

TINY TIM:

The crippled son of Bob Cratchit in Dickens' "A Christmas Carol," who Ebenezer Scrooge befriends when he discovers he wants to change the way he has been living his life.

TOM AND JERRY:

In the northwest of England, it was a custom to welcome a newborn baby by mixing a rum butter sauce and pouring it over cakes or scones. The sauce was made from rum, butter, sugar, and nutmeg and was called a Cumberland sauce. The ingredients stood for the following:

RUM	The spirit of life
SUGAR	The sweetness of life
BUTTER	The goodness of life
NUTMEG	The spice of life

These are the same ingredients used in a Tom and Jerry and in an eggnog with the addition of eggs and milk. This is a popular Christmas drink.[8]

TREE TOPPERS:

The name given to the ornament at the top of the Christmas tree. Usually it depicts a design of the Star of Bethlehem or an angel. In some homes it is a tradition to pass the tree topper to the oldest child on their 15th Christmas.

TRIFLE:

An English dessert consisting of sponge cake soaked in wine, spread with jam, and covered with custard. It has become a traditional holiday dessert in England.

T

TURKEY:

The turkey came to England from America in 1542. It replaced exotic fowl as the traditional holiday entree, such as swans, peacocks, and bustards.[9] During the time of Dickens, it was very expensive and therefore a very special gift to the Cratchits.

TWELVE DAYS OF CHRISTMAS:

The winter solstice festivities lasted for several weeks. The Saxon King, Alfred, decreed that Christmas should last from December 25th to

Epiphany on January 6th. No one was to work during this time so that the teachings of the church could be carried out. During the reign of King Henry the VIII, tradesmen were encouraged to play games during these twelve days. They were allowed to gamble which was against the law at any other time of the year. These were the bawdiest of Christmas times.

THE TWELVE DAYS (SONG):

The Twelve Days of Christmas was a popular rhyme in New England in the 1800s. Its origins were from Medieval times and it is an example of Medieval numerological wit. Since the giver gives one gift on the first day (a partridge in a pear tree) and three on the second day (two turtle doves and a partridge in a pear tree) by the end of the song he has given 364 gifts, one for every day of the year but one.[10]

THE TWELFTH NIGHT:

The finish of the Christmas season was held on January 6th, the twelfth night of Christmas or Epiphany. It was a feast to end all feasts. It ended with a dessert known as the twelfth night cake, today known as the fruit cake! Before it was baked, a bean and a pea were buried in the cake. The man who found the bean became the King for the evening and the woman who found the pea became the Queen. Once they had been chosen, the party began and they were in charge of the festivities. Games were played, one of the most popular being "charades." After the party, the Christmas decorations were taken down. It was thought to be unlucky if the decorations were taken down on or before January 6th.[11]

V

VIRGIN BIRTH:

The birth of Jesus Christ, as told in the New Testament, tells of the virginal conception of Mary by the Holy Spirit. Belief that Christ was conceived without a human father was universally accepted in the church by the 2nd century. A virgin birth is not only found in the Christian religions, but also in the Jewish religion with the birth of Isaac, and the other ancient pagan religions.

VIRGINIA:

A girl name Virginia, later known as Mrs. Laura Virginia O'Hanlon, wondered why some of her friends did not believe in Santa Claus. She was eight years old. When she asked her father and he was evasive with his answer, she decided to write to The New York Sun newspaper and ask them if there was a Santa Claus. Her father had always said that if it appeared in the Sun, it had to be true. Her letter was answered by Francis Church, a writer for the Sun who specialized in controversial subjects. His wonderful answer appeared in the Sun on September 21st, 1897 entitled "Yes Virginia, There is a Santa."

W

WASSAIL:

An ancient toast or expression of good will during a festive occasion. It was also an ale used on special occasions, such as Christmas caroling.

W

WHITE CHRISTMAS:

This Christmas song was written by Irving Berlin and sung in 1942 by Bing Crosby in the movie "Holiday Inn." The copyrights to this song are the most valuable in the world.

WINDOW CANDLES:

A candle placed in a window is an old Irish custom. Candles were placed in windows at twilight on Christmas Eve and were to burn during the twelve nights of Christmas. They were placed there as a guide for Mary and Joseph so they would be able to find their way. People have now replaced these candles with electric lighted candles.

WINTER SOLSTICE:

The Winter solstice is on December 21st and is the shortest day of the year. People have celebrated this season by lighting fires to the gods to make the sun last for another year. The Vikings celebrated the Yuletide by lighting great bonfires. This was to insure good crops for the following year. The Persians built fires on December 25th to worship their god of light, Mythra. The Egyptians honored Iris, the mother of their sun god, Horis. The Romans celebrated with the feast to Saturnalia, by feasting and gift giving. They lit candles and decorated with evergreens.

W

WREATH:

Part of many ancient traditions was to bring evergreens indoors during the time of the winter solstice as a symbol of life. People in Egypt, the middle Orient, and Europe, all had wreaths, as did the ancient Romans. In England, before the advent of the Christmas tree, a circular bough of evergreens was brought into the house on Christmas Eve. It was decorated with candles, apples, paper decorations, ornaments, and mistletoe. If a girl was standing under the wreath with mistletoe, she was entitled to a kiss. A man was entitled to as many kisses as there were berries in the mistletoe.

X

XMAS:

X in the Greek alphabet stands for Christ; therefore, an abbreviated way to write Christmas is XMAS.

Y

YORKSHIRE PUDDING:

A batter of flour, eggs, and milk baked in the juices of roasted meat. Originally it was made by the poorer classes who wanted the taste of meat but could not afford it. Now it has become a part of a traditional English Holiday dinner.

YULE:

The name the Vikings gave the season at the time of the winter solstice.

YULELOG:

The main log used in the fire at Yuletide. Later it became the main log in the Christmas Eve fire. It was thought to be good luck to keep the fire going for the twelve days of Christmas and to save a piece of the yulelog to start next year's fire.

A
CHRISTMAS
TIME LINE

CHRISTMAS TIME LINE

The "winter solstice" is worshipped by ancient cultures on December 21st. The Vikings had the Yule. The Persians, the worship of Mythra, their god of light. The Egyptians honored Iris, the mother of their sun god. The Romans had Saturnalia, a feast with gift giving and evergreens. The Jews had Hanukkah, the feast of lights, although this is not a winter solstice celebration.

Approximately from 500 to 1650 Christmas festivities are at their peak. Bawdy parties, Misrule, bawdy Christmas carols, and feasts beyond the imagination are the rule at Christmas celebrations.

1200 BC	Druids and Vikings celebrate the winter solstice around December 22nd
274 BC	Romans celebrate the feast of the "Invincible Sun" on December 25th
0 AD	Christ is born
02 AD	Mary and Joseph return to Nazareth
33 AD	Christ dies
66 AD	Druids and Celts defeated by the Romans
336 AD	Pope Julius starts to celebrate Christmas on Dec. 25th
350 AD	St. Nicholas is a bishop in Russia
350 AD	The Christmas stocking tradition begins
500 AD	Pope Gregory declares December 25th as Christ's birth
532 AD	Monk Dionysius Exgius starts Christian dating system
550 AD	Pope Gregory asks that archbishop Augustine in England convert pagan customs to Christmas
649 AD	The church establishes the "Immaculate Conception"
1224 AD	St. Francis of Assisi introduces the "CRECHE"
1300 AD	Mystery plays flourish
1300 AD	Christmas carols come to England from France
1350 AD	Boxing Day starts
1542 AD	The first turkey is imported into England
1648 AD	Cromwell comes to power and the Puritans rule

Cromwell gains power in 1648 and the reign of the Puritans begins. They discourage Christmas for the next 200 years, from 1650 to 1850, until the reign of Queen Victoria. Churches are closed and stores are made to stay open on Christmas.

1700 AD	Plum pudding becomes popular
1824 AD	Clement Moore writes "A Visit from St. Nick"
1832 AD	The first tree in the U.S. is decorated in Boston
1841 AD	Queen Victoria has a Christmas tree in Windsor Castle
1843 AD	Charles Dickens writes "A Christmas Carol"
1843 AD	John Horsley prints the first Christmas card
1850 AD	Christmas gifts become a tradition
1850 AD	Christmas crackers are invented by Thomas Smith
1852 AD	Dr. Joel Poinsette brings the poinsettia to the U.S.
1854 AD	Pope Pius IX declares Mary to be free of original sin
1856 AD	President Pierce has the first White House Christmas tree
1857 AD	Gift giving becomes a tradition at Christmas
1860 AD	Christmas trees are now a tradition
1880 AD	The Santa Claus myth is firmly established
1885 AD	Glass ornaments are exported from Germany to the U.S.
1882 AD	Tchaikovsky writes the "Nutcracker" ballet
1887 AD	Francis Church writes "Yes Virginia, There is a Santa"
1888 AD	Electric Christmas lights are invented
1900 AD	Commercial Christmas stockings become available
1906 AD	T. Roosevelt helps make the Christmas tree a crop
1909 AD	First Public Christmas tree on Mt. Wilson in California
1919 AD	Madison Square Garden has a public tree
1920 AD	Red Christmas window wreaths become popular
1925 AD	Pres. Coolidge has 1st Christmas tree on White House lawn
1942 AD	Bing Crosby makes "White Christmas" popular
1949 AD	Gene Autry sings "Rudolph, the Red Nosed Reindeer"
1951 AD	Pope Pius XII makes an official doctrine that Mary is free of original sin
1952 AD	Outside Christmas lights become popular
1955 AD	Bubble lights make their appearance
1955 AD	Aluminum Christmas trees become popular
1970 AD	Artificial evergreen trees become popular
1978 AD	Miniature Christmas tree lights replace large bulbs
1995 AD	Peter Harrington writes "Christmas Treevia"

FOOTNOTES

1. JENNIE REEKIE, *THE LONDON RITZ BOOK OF CHRISTMAS*, LONDON, 1989, P. 10.

2. ASTRID HENKELS & JAMES BEAUDRY, *THE SATURDAY EVENING POST CHRISTMAS BOOK*, INDIANAPOLIS, 1978, P. 118.

3. JENNIE REEKIE, *THE LONDON RITZ BOOK OF CHRISTMAS*, LONDON, 1989, P. 31-32.

4. JENNIE REEKIE, *THE LONDON RITZ BOOK OF CHRISTMAS*, LONDON, 1989, P. 30.

5. IRENA CHALMERS, *THE GREAT AMERICAN CHRISTMAS ALMANAC*, NEW YORK, 1989, P. 189.

6. JENNIE REEKIE, *THE LONDON RITZ BOOK OF CHRISTMAS*, LONDON, 1989, P. 12.

7. HERBERT H. WERNECKE, *CHRISTMAS CUSTOMS AROUND THE WORLD*, PHILADELPHIA, 1988, P. 35.

8. JENNIE REEKIE, *THE LONDON RITZ BOOK OF CHRISTMAS*, LONDON, 1989, P. 33.

9. JENNIE REEKIE, *THE LONDON RITZ BOOK OF CHRISTMAS*, LONDON, 1989, P. 27.

10. HENNIG COHEN AND FRISTRAM POTTER COFFIN, *THE FOLKLORE OF AMERICAN HOLIDAYS*, DETROIT & LONDON, 1989, P. 474-475.

11. JENNIE REEKIE, *THE LONDON RITZ BOOK OF CHRISTMAS*, LONDON, 1989, P. 19.

NOTES

NOTES